Deciding Well

Deciding Well

A Christian Perspective
on Making Decisions as a Leader

Peter Shaw CB

REGENT COLLEGE PUBLISHING
Vancouver, British Columbia

Dedicated to Jim and Rita Houston and
to Ward and Laurel Gasque who for nearly
forty years have been a wonderful source
of encouragement, challenge
and inspiration

Published 2009 by Regent College Publishing
5800 University Boulevard, Vancouver, BC V6T 2E4 Canada
Web: www.regentpublishing.com
E-mail: info@regentpublishing.com

Book design by Robert Hand
<roberthandcommunications.com>

Regent College Publishing is an imprint of the Regent Bookstore
<www.regentbookstore.com>. Views expressed in works published by Regent
College Publishing are those of the author and do not necessarily represent the
official position of Regent College <www.regent-college.edu>.

ISBN-13: 978-1-57383-436-0
ISBN-10: 1-57383-436-X

A cataloguing record for this book is available
from Library and Archives Canada Cataloguing in Publication

Contents

Acknowledgments

The two prompts for this book were the commission from John Wiley to write a leadership book entitled *Making Difficult Decisions: How to be Decisive and Get the Business Done* and leading a one week summer school at Regent College in Vancouver on 'The Christian Leader in the Secular World of Work'. Part of the summer school course was about how Christians are best equipped to make hard decisions. I was delighted to have the opportunity to turn an initial paper for that course into this short book.

When I was one of the first four fulltime students at Regent College in 1970 the encouragement and challenge from Jim Houston, the Principal, and Ward Gasque, a member of the faculty, were so important in stretching my thinking about aiming to bring a Christian perspective into the work environment. The encouragement from Jim and Rita Houston and Ward and Laurel Gasque has been very important over a period of nearly forty years.

I am grateful to Sally Smith who originally commissioned me to write the book *Making Difficult Decisions* and to Sarah Sutton for allowing me to draw from sections of that book in this text. I am grateful to Rod Wilson and Don Lewis who asked me to teach the summer school course at Regent College.

The thoughts in the book have come out of conversations with colleagues and clients in different spheres. Many one-to-one coaching sessions have covered difficult decisions. I have had the privilege of leading workshops on this subject in both the public, private and voluntary sectors and on four continents. I am grateful for the stimulus and thinking that has come from my colleagues at Praesta Partners.

Rodney Green and Dave Brockman have provided valuable comments on a first draft. Rob Clements, Robert Hand and Bill Reimer from Regent College Publishing have been an important source of practical help. Ann Collins has provided valuable typing support while Claire Pratt has arranged my diary with great skill to ensure that I have been able to balance a range of different commitments while putting this short book together.

Frances and our children Graham, Ruth and Colin have always been great companions and have given wise advice when I have needed to make hard decisions.

I am grateful for John Pritchard, the Bishop of Oxford, for writing the foreword. John has a special gift of bringing wisdom alongside human empathy and sensitivity, together with awareness of the importance of living the Christian Gospel in the way we live our lives and make decisions.

I was invited to speak at a service at a recent Regent College reunion and spoke about the words of Jesus, 'be as wise as serpents and as innocent as doves'. This phrase encapsulated Jesus' approach to making decisions and provides a useful framework for all decisions. Decision making is about drawing from our intellectual, physical, emotional and spiritual awareness. At the heart of good decision making is being open-minded and yet rooted in our Christian values. It is my hope that this short book will provide a practical stimulus to developing your capacity to make decisions in human terms and to develop the perspective you bring as a Christian to making hard decisions.

Peter Shaw
peteralanshaw@gmail.com
Godalming, England
March 2009

Foreword

It's tempting to try and make hard decisions in the spirit of the old adage, 'When you come to a fork in the road, take it'. Many of us would like to be able to avoid the hard decisions that come with leadership because we know they risk disaster or making us unpopular. Peter Shaw, on the other hand, seeks to persuade us that being called to make such decisions is a privilege, and the ability to make such decisions is a gift—a gift we can develop. It is in that spirit that Peter invites us to explore a Christian perspective on making these hard choices.

As I make the kind of decisions Peter writes about I keep in the back of my mind a cartoon I once saw with the members of a church council sitting around a table. The vicar is summing up. 'So', he says, 'the vote is as follows: Eric, Ruth, Tim, Peter and Jenny are *for* the proposal. God and I are against'. The cartoon nicely illustrates the danger for Christian leaders of calling to their side the very highest of authorities and bolting divine sanction onto their pet ideas.

My own experience chimes in much more readily with the wise suggestions offered by Peter Shaw. He demonstrates what we can learn from the practice of Jesus, from the wisdom of good secular practice, and from particular Christian thinkers. He asks the hard questions about hard questions—and answers them. He offers ten clear steps to develop our capacity to make difficult decisions in human terms, and then ten clear steps to develop our Christian perspective on the task. It's all admirably laid out, although Peter would be the first to say that the process is unavoidably messy in practice. But then isn't the Holy Spirit much less tidy than we would like?

What emerges is a form of what earlier theologians would have called *habitus*, a disposition of the heart that includes the head and represents a synergy of prayer, study and experience. It is in this holistic mix of shrewdness and innocence that Godly wisdom lies.

Peter brings over thirty years of significant experience to this study. As a Director General in Government Departments, an Executive Coach, a Visiting Professor of Leadership Development at Newcastle University Business School, and a valued writer and speaker, as well as a reader and long-time Christian, he brings a unique range of skills and narratives to the task. He writes with commendable clarity, understanding well the needs of the busy Christian leader. He writes with insight and illustration. Above all, he writes with encouragement and hope. I have known Peter for many years and have always been impressed by the way he blends the values of his faith with the highest professional standards at work. What we have available in this book is the breadth and length of that maturity.

Sometimes I am tempted to think that the secret of making good decisions is the experience of making bad ones, and I know I have made plenty of those. I would have been much better prepared for the fray had I had on my desk Peter's new book. Read it and benefit!

+John Pritchard, Bishop of Oxford

Introduction

Why is this decision so hard? We wrestle with different ways of looking at a decision without making much progress. The issue seems to get more complicated and not simpler. We sometimes want to bash our head against the wall with frustration. We want to cry out, 'Where is God in this'!

But then a way forward may become clearer—sometimes it is in a very different direction, while at other times we feel a new sense of peace about a direction we had explored once before. Sometimes there is no clarity about next steps and we have to decide, or reconcile ourselves to staying in a place of indecision or searching.

As Christians we are called upon to make hard decisions, especially so when we have leadership responsibilities. Being a Christian does not make these decisions easier, as we can often see many different angles to the same issue. Our Christian faith does not protect us from hard decisions or allow us just to dump them on God. Our Creator God gave us brains to reason with, emotions to help us understand and an awareness of the needs of individuals.

Tough decisions come in many different shapes and sizes. For any leader or manager there are decisions covering strategic direction, resourcing, priorities, communications and the management of staff. In a church or Christian organisation there is likely to be the further dimension of participants having strong personal views and the additional joy and complication of working with volunteers.

This book draws inspiration and practical lessons from the approach of Jesus to making decisions. It then looks at wider evidence about what makes a good decision maker before considering what is distinctive about Christian discernment in making decisions.

Against this background the book aims to help you reflect on your approach to decision making and to develop an approach which is rooted in both biblical truth and practical reality. It then reflects on possibly ways of addressing specific choices.

The final chapter is designed to help you to develop your capacity to make hard decisions by encouraging you to draw ever more effectively on your own practical experience, your experience of Christian faith, your theological understanding, the richness of other peoples' experience and the approaches that work best for you. The aim is to develop in you those elusive and precious skills of discernment which will enable you to make hard decisions well in a variety of different contexts, whether at work, at home, in your community or in your church.

My hope is that this book will be of value to individuals, small groups that look at the book one chapter at a time and discuss the questions in each chapter, and larger groups that might use the workshop outline in the appendix.

I

Jesus' Approach
to Making Decisions

Our starting point is the way Jesus made decisions. How willing was he to make decisions? What sort of decisions did he make and how did he approach those decisions?

The Gospels record Jesus making many different types of decisions. He made hard decisions when he left home to be an itinerant preacher, picked his disciples, chose who to disagree with and where to pitch the level of controversy, chose to go to Jerusalem leading to his crucifixion and faced interrogation between Gethsemane and his crucifixion.

Some of the features of his decision making were:

- *boldness*—he was willing to set out a clear way forward, even if others did not agree; he was willing to take risks and ready to incur the scepticism or disagreement of others;
- *commitment*—he stuck with his choice of disciples even though they exasperated him at times by their slowness to learn and lack of courage;

- *resoluteness*—there was a resolve in the way he made decisions and stuck with them; he set his face towards Jerusalem knowing that it would lead to his crucifixion and was not deterred from this intent;
- *clarity*—Jesus did not hide who he was or the nature of his calling; he was unequivocal and consistent under questioning or interrogation, although sometimes the clarity was only fully clear with the benefit of hindsight.

Some of the characteristics of the way Jesus handled hard decisions include the following. There was clarity of purpose which provided a framework for his hard decisions. He understood the wider context of both state and church politics as he talked and listened with leaders and understood where they were coming from. He retained his ability to be compassionate and express his own humanity even when he was making hard decisions. He sought opportunities to withdraw and reflect. He was willing to make the decisions only he could make and was prepared to live by the decisions he had made. Jesus would sometimes prepare for hard decisions by spending an entire night in prayer.

When he made hard decisions Jesus drew on a range of different forms of awareness. He embodied

- *physical awareness,* by being with people at close quarters;
- *emotional awareness,* by understanding their needs, hopes and fears;
- *intellectual awareness,* through his discussion and debating of issues and his telling of parables to stretch his hearers' thinking; and

- *spiritual awareness,* by understanding their deepest needs for forgiveness, new life and hope.

Jesus had a remarkable ability to combine these four different aspects of awareness when talking with individuals. For example, as he spoke with the Samaritan woman at the well there was both physical presence, awareness of her particular emotional needs, discussion with her on an intellectual level about the significance of water and a spiritual awareness of her need to worship the Father in spirit and truth.

Jesus was both the Son of God and a human leader. Therefore reflecting on his approach to decisions brings an awareness of both God's purposes expressed through Jesus as the Son of God and an awareness of the best of thoughtful human leadership.

In my book *Mirroring Jesus as Leader* I suggested that the main characteristics of Jesus' leadership can be summed up in the six themes of Jesus as visionary, servant, teacher, coach, radical and healer. These characteristics impact the way Jesus made decisions and encouraged others to do so:

- as *visionary* Jesus encouraged his followers to focus on decisions that reflected the Kingdom of God;
- as *servant* he listened to others and showed generosity of spirit when decisions were to be made;
- as *teacher* he used stories and parables to enable his hearers to think about their world in a different way and thereby bring a new perspective to decision making;
- as *coach* he developed the capacities of his disciples and others to become leaders able to make decisions in the future through their experience of discipleship;

- as *radical* he 'spoke truth unto power' and was direct in his words and actions, showing a decisiveness in controversial situations; and
- as *healer* he brought physical, emotional and spiritual healing where helplessness was replaced with hope for the future, thereby creating a positive context within which decisions could be made.

When discussing the themes above with a wide range of people two clear additional characteristics have frequently been referred to. These are *availability* and *patience*. Jesus was available to a wide range of different people. He stopped to talk to the woman who touched the hem of his garment. He met with Zacchaeus. When the crowds followed him he spent time with them. Jesus made sure that he had periods when he was alone or just with his disciples, but he was regularly available to a wider group to listen, talk and heal. This theme of availability is pertinent to decision making because it ensures a full understanding of the concerns and perceptions of individuals who will be impacted by a decision.

Jesus was both bold and patient. In his book *The Fourfold Leadership of Jesus*, Andrew Watson, bishop of Aston, writes of Jesus' 'wait for me' leadership involving powerful expectancy, pro-activity, patience and endurance. Watson writes of Jesus never appearing rushed or hurried. He comments that looking from a place of rest is quite different to resting from the place of work.

> In terms of endurance 'wait for me' leadership involves a recognition that waiting itself can have real value in developing perseverance, character, hope and Godly maturity. The thirty days in the wilderness was a time of

discipline, endurance, patience and above all trust build-ing.

For Watson a sense of waiting is not like the inactivity of the two tramps in *Waiting for Godot,* who fill their days with increasingly meaningless chatter as they wait for someone who might save them and fulfil their lives.

> Nothing could be further removed from the biblical call to 'wait for the Lord' or from the faith-filled expectancy that lies at its heart. Waiting in this sense is both an expression of our dependence on God and a recognition that his timing is not always our timing. If we are to live (and lead) properly we must do so for the longer term rather than seeking first a quick win and a popularity that will evaporate as quickly as it has materialised.

When I facilitated a course recently at Regent College in Vancouver on the theme of the Christian leader in the secular world of work, perspectives of participants on the approach of Jesus to making decisions included the centrality he attached to prayer, his purposeful contemplation and dialoguing with his Father; the clarity of purpose he brought to decisions; the confidence with which he made decisions; his awareness of the physical and emotional needs of individuals; the impact of his sense of timing in making decisions; and the clarity of his identity and purpose expressed through his decisions.

One participant on that course distinguished between the major decisions Jesus made and consequential decisions. Some of the major decisions may have been hard, with others flowing naturally from the initial hard decision. Once Jesus had made the choice to go to Jerusalem prior to his crucifixion, the decisions during the subsequent week may have been consequential rather than hard in themselves. The practical application may be about identifying the key decisions which, once made, will make consequential decisions more straight-forward.

As Wise as Serpents and as Innocent as Doves

Many of the words Jesus used have an impact on the way we make decisions. A phrase that has particular relevance to decision making is the advice to the disciples to 'be as wise as serpents and as innocent as doves' (Matt. 10:16). This phrase encapsulates Jesus' approach. At a theatre in London recently I was looked firmly in the eye by C. S. Lewis. He was peering down from a great height and looking rather severely at me. The venue was a production of *Shadowlands*, which is about the marriage of C. S. Lewis and Joy Davidson. The play was about to begin and Charles Dance, the actor playing C. S. Lewis, walked on. A mobile phone went off close to where I was sitting. It was not my phone; it was the phone of my immediate neighbour! But Charles Dance frowned at me se-verely, perhaps because I was in a suit and looked as if I was a prime suspect. I tried to look as 'innocent as a dove' but on this occasion my innocence did not appear to cut any ice!

In *Mere Christianity* C. S. Lewis reflects on these words of Jesus':

> Christ never meant that we were to remain children in intelligence: on the contrary. He told us to be not only 'as harmless as doves', but also as wise as serpents. He wants a child's heart, but a grown-up's head. He wants us to be simple, single-minded, affectionate, and teachable, as good children are; but He also wants every bit of intel-ligence we have to be alert at its job, and in first-class fighting trim. The fact that what you are thinking about is God Himself (for example, when you are praying) does

not mean that you can be content with the same babyish ideas which you had when you were a five-year-old.

C. S. Lewis challenged his readers to hold that balance of a child's heart and a grown-up's head—the balance between being simple, single-minded and affectionate, alongside using every bit of intelligence that is available to us.

What is the context for this verse in Matthew? Chapter 10 is the turning point in the gospel. The first nine chapters have been full of wonderful teaching. The reader has now learnt of John's baptism and Jesus' baptism, heard the Sermon on the Mount, observed the faith of the centurion, learnt of Jesus calming the storm and the accounts of the healing ministry of Jesus. But now we move into a new act in the drama. It is time for the disciples to be sent out.

The initial phase of listening and observing moves into the disciples being given responsibility to 'go out'. They are told to 'go, preach this message: The kingdom of heaven is near'. Jesus says to them 'freely you have received, freely give'. They are told to greet people and bring peace, but where they are not welcomed, they are to shake the dust off their feet. Jesus cautions them that he is sending them out like sheep among wolves. So the context for the text is very clear, as the disciples set out into a potentially hostile world, they are to be as wise as serpents and as innocent as doves.

In his commentary on Matthew, R. T. France suggests that the word 'wise' stands for sensible or prudent actions:

> Christians are not to be gullible simpletons. But neither are they to be rogues. Innocent is literally 'unmixed', i.e., pure, transparent; it demands not naivety, but an irreproachable honesty. The balance of prudence and purity

will enable Christians both to survive and to fulfil their mission to the world.

Another commentary refers to innocence meaning 'unmixed' or 'without guile'. For me, 'without guile' sums up so much in this text. Innocence is not about naivety but about honesty and openness, with no hint of duplicity or guile.

In *Matthew for Everyone*, N. T. Wright includes a helpful paragraph about this text:

> Faced with this awesome challenge, Jesus' sharp advice to his followers was: be shrewd like snakes, but innocent like doves. Christians often find it easy to be one or the other, but seldom both. Without innocence, shrewdness becomes manipulative; without shrewdness, innocence becomes naivety. Though we face different crises and different problems to those of the first disciples, we still need that finely balanced character, reflecting so remarkably that of Jesus himself. If we are in any way to face what he faced, and to share his work, we need to be sure that his own life becomes embodied in ours.

Wright refers to that finely balanced character of holding together wisdom and shrewdness alongside innocence that is not naivety. Shrewdness and innocence provide a valuable framework for decision making. Shrewdness—being discerning, prudent, perceptive and clear-headed. Innocence—bringing generosity of heart, compassion, understanding, listening, openness and honesty. The phrase challenges us to think about the wisdom, shrewdness and prudence that God has grown in us and how we might use those special gifts of listening, talking, writing, giving and loving God has given us. Through continuous learning, giving, serving and exploring, how might God grow, challenge and cherish those gifts in us? It is not just about being wise, it is being innocent too. It means practising an innocence which is open to fresh experiences of God's grace, open to new conversations, new insights and new people so we are receptive to new freshness and vitality in our pilgrimage of faith and life.

This text provides a framework for looking at hard decisions and encouraging us to come at issues in ways in which we are as wise as serpents and as innocent as doves. Many of Jesus' statements provide a valuable context for reflecting on decisions. The following are of fourteen statements from Matthew's Gospel, each one of which can help us view decisions we are about to make in a different way:

- Give unto Caesar what is Caesar's and unto God what is God's.
- Blessed are the peacemakers, for they will be called the sons of God.
- You are the salt of the earth.
- You are the light of the world.
- Blessed are the pure in heart for they will see God.
- Blessed are the meek for they will inherit the earth.
- Love your enemies and pray for those who persecute you.
- Ask and it will be given to you; seek and you will find; knock and the door will be opened to you.
- Do not judge, or you too will be judged.
- Do not worry about your life, what you eat or drink, or about your body, what you will wear.
- Seek first the kingdom and his righteousness, and all the things will be given to you as well.
- If you do not forgive others their sins, your Father will not forgive your sins.
- Watch out for false prophets.

- Come to me all you who are weary and burdened and I will give you a rest.

Reflecting on one of Jesus' statements above, cognisant of the context in which it was used, can bring new clarity to our own thinking in a particular situation.

Conclusion

Each time we read a story about Jesus or an account of the words he spoke there can be new insights into the way he listened to others, developed their thinking and experience, and prepared them for decisions they would need to make. Rereading the Gospels and looking for perspectives which speak to the circumstances in which we find ourselves can provide a source of continued new freshness. This is provided we allow the words of Jesus to speak anew to us in a wide range of different situations where decisions need to be made.

Questions to ask yourself might be:

- What do you see as distinctive in the way Jesus approached decisions?
- How significant for you is Jesus' phrase 'be as wise as serpents and as innocent as doves'?
- What phrases from Jesus' teaching are relevant to the decisions that you are needing to make?

2

What Makes a Good
Decision Maker?

This chapter looks at the elements of what makes for good decision making. After looking at a selection of views it considers the place of clarity, conviction, courage and communication.

I often invite people in pairs to think of someone they respect as a good decision maker and identify three characteristics or behaviours that provide evidence that they are a good decision maker. There is often a surprising degree of consensus.

When I asked this question of a group of leaders recently in Vancouver they commented that leaders who make good decisions

- do sound reflection and analysis;
- are clear about the big picture;
- are honest thinkers trying to seek truth and the best way forward;
- bring practical experience and are self aware about their own reaction and the reaction of others;

- are able to bring and articulate a clear vision and are guided by clear principles;
- weigh options and then stick to the decision they have made;
- are able to evaluate options looking at the long term;
- are willing to talk to a range of different people;
- are willing to revise their approach if there are major changes—admitting that adjustments are needed is not regarded as a sense of failure;
- can see different perspectives;
- are clear about the consequences of different approaches and actions;
- are willing to trust people to take decisions forward; and
- are willing to stay around long enough to see the consequences of their decisions.

When I led a weekend training event on leadership with curates in a UK Midlands Anglican Diocese we looked at the characteristics of hard leadership decisions. The shared view was that hard decisions often had the following characteristics:

- there could be unpredictable side effects;
- there may be consequences which will be difficult to handle involving people who might be hurt;
- others may not have a full perspective and may react adversely because they do not know or cannot know the full picture;
- the balance between what is right and what is pragmatic may be difficult and unstable;
- some hard decisions may mean challenging traditional authority which is unlikely to be popular;

- sometimes you can feel between a 'rock' and a 'hard place' when there is no obviously right answer and each option will lead to difficulties;
- hard decisions might lead to a reaction of personal criticism which will be painful;
- there will be dilemmas about when to persevere with a particular course of action and when to be flexible because of the views of others; and
- communicating a hard decision effectively may seem so difficult to do well that the validity of the decision is called into question.

Clarity, Conviction, Courage and Communication

When I wrote *Making Difficult Decisions: How to be Decisive and Get the Business Done* I drew from discussions with a wide range of people in leadership positions in the private, public and voluntary sectors. What came out of this research was that whatever the nature of the decisions an individual or organisation is making, the principles of good decision making are the same. Good decision making is all about

- *clarity*—utter objectivity about the issue, the context, the risks and the consequences;
- *conviction*—the place of intuition, values and judgement based on experience;
- *courage*—turning belief into action to build next steps; and
- *communication*—embracing listening, engaging and persuading.

The heart of good decision making is balancing clarity and conviction. It is the interplay between analysis and beliefs, between logical thinking and the 'gut' reaction that is at the heart of how we make good decisions. Courage and communication are the essential elements to being decisive, taking forward difficult decisions effectively and reaching outcomes.

The book *Making Difficult Decisions* includes a wide range of examples of leaders balancing clarity and conviction including high court judges, a chief constable, medical consultant, prison governor, and a government minister as well as chief executives in the construction, aeronautical engineering and food and drink industries. Each leader wrested with the best way of balancing clarity and conviction. They all saw hard decisions as a necessary part of their jobs; they had to draw on all their sources of insight, using their brains and hearts as sources of valuable input.

Our ability to make hard decisions depends partly on our self-understanding and how we handle ourselves when making decisions. We need to know when we are good at making decisions and when we are in danger of being less effective because of blinkering, avoidance, vulnerability or even fear. Understanding our own strengths and weaknesses is essential to our being able to improve our ability to make good decisions and move on. Understanding the way other people make decisions provides important input, especially those people whose styles and preferences are very different from our own.

A key starting point for any decision making is *clarity*. Time spent clarifying the issue and then working through the analysis is rarely wasted. It is a matter of maintaining momentum, keeping up the resolve to get to clarity about the way ahead and acknowledging when to crystallise options and when to compromise.

The critical steps of clarity include the following:

- *being clear about the issue,* which involves being objective about the elements, defining the problem and being clear on the context;
- *doing the analysis,* which means ensuring sound reasoning, living with complexity, ensuring sound structure and processes and doing thorough risk analysis; and
- *taking a clear way forward,* which requires focused objectives, defining clear options, knowing when to compromise, triangulating your views with others, working through consequences, striving for simplicity and being aware of the pitfalls.

Conviction comes from a number of different sources such as intuitive judgment, the relevance of values, the significance of past experience, trained judgment and emotional awareness.

Conviction can be criticised as non-objective, prejudice or a means of escape from reality. Testing whether a conviction is helpful or dangerous is crucial or else we fall into a spiral of self-deception. Conviction is an asset when based on good understanding, but it needs to be accompanied by honesty and the ability to analyse your own thinking. If conviction becomes blinkered dogma it can blind us to reality. Conviction needs to be continually assessed and tested. Experience from good leaders suggests that the approaches individuals use to test the significance of their convictions include standing back, keeping calm, conversing with colleagues, mentoring and coaching, and being aware of pitfalls.

From the evidence of talking to a wide range of leaders *courage* in taking decisions forward needs to be deep seated; it involves being comfortable with your own values, addressing your fears, being willing to be bold when you feel strongly about an issue, knowing what happens if you are courageous, recognising and enjoying the courage of others and learning from their approaches. Courage also comes from being curious; asking the right questions and probing; identifying risks and being clear how significant they are; thinking clearly about what the right next steps might be; and taking a stand if a course of action is clearly unfair and counterproductive in its treatment of individuals. It can mean not going with the flow sometimes when key facts are being ignored or misinterpreted.

The essential elements of courage when taking hard decisions can be:

- *action*—turn belief into action, build clear next steps, and have the courage to act;
- *reflection*—consider where compassion and coherence fit in, be aware of the consequences and be ready to live with ambiguity; and
- *ensure progress*—decide how best to overcome your fears, build in feedback, build in resilience, learn from mistakes, stay focused and be aware of pitfalls.

Effective *communication* is essential in any decision making process. Good communication is not just the effective communication of the outcome, it is a process from start to finish that involves listening, building partnerships, effective engagement, creating consensus and effective persuasion prior to the point when decisions need to be made.

With any decision-making process a key initial step is understanding the context and being able to understand the perspective of others. Effective communication of the outcome is one of the last steps, although reflection throughout the process on how a decision is going to be communicated is an invaluable test when looking at the potential realism of a particular decision. Essential elements of communication during hard decisions include:

- *building understanding*—keep listening, build partnerships, and ensure effective engagement;
- *building agreement*—which includes persuasion that works, building consensus, seeking agreement, reflecting on the timing and ensuring adequate information is available; and
- *taking action*—communicate the outcome, be clear on the rationale, watch the cultural interpretation, have a sound feedback loop and be aware of the pitfalls.

In summary, the experience from effective leaders suggests that when you are handling a forthcoming demanding decision key questions to ask yourself are:

Clarity

- Are you adequately clear about the issue, the problem and the context?
- Is there enough analysis available with proper account taken of risks?
- Are there ways forward with objectives and options and thought-through consequences?

Conviction

- What are your intuitive reactions, values, past experiences, distilled experiences and emotional awareness telling you?
- Can you test your developing convictions through standing back, keeping calm and talking it through with a colleague, a mentor and your coach?

Courage

- How easy is it to turn belief into action and have the courage to act?
- Have you had the opportunity to reflect on where compassion or coherence fit in?
- Are there ways you can best ensure progress through overcoming fears, building in feedback and resilience, and learning from mistakes?

Communication

- Can you build greater understanding through listening, building partnerships and ensuring effective engagement?
- Are there further steps needed towards building agreement through persuasion or building consensus?
- What focus might there be on further action which involves communicating the outcomes, clarity of rationale, watching the cultural interpretation and having a sound feedback loop?

What is often most difficult is balancing clarity and conviction when decisions have to be made on the basis of limited information or at speed.

A Christian perspective impacts the four principles above in the following illustrative ways:

- *clarity*—the obligation to be honest, straight, factual and full of integrity;
- *conviction*—the place of the Christian tenets that individuals can be reborn and grow, with compassion, forgiveness and hope playing an important part;

- *courage*—where living our values and mirroring Jesus as a visionary, servant teacher, coach, radical and healer can be helpful; and
- *communication*—where following Jesus' example of constantly listening and engaging has such a valuable place.

Smart Choices

As an example of another approach to making decisions, in their book entitled *Smart Choices: A Practical Guide to Making Better Life Decisions*, John Hammond, Ralph Keeney and Howard Raiffa talk of effective decision-making processes fulfilling six criteria:

- it focuses on what is important;
- it is logical and consistent;
- it acknowledges both subjective and objective factors and blends analytical with intuitive thinking;
- it requires only as much information and analysis as is necessary to resolve a particular dilemma;
- it encourages and guides the gathering of relevant information and informed opinion; and
- it is straightforward, reliable, easy to use and flexible.

The authors see addressing these criteria as being relevant for decisions that are either major or minor. They suggest eight keys to effective decision making:

- work on the right problem;
- specify your objectives;
- create imaginative alternatives;

- understand the consequences;
- grapple with your trade-offs;
- clarify your uncertainties;
- think hard about your risk tolerance; and
- consider linked decisions.

The authors set out a very rational approach to dealing with a range of different practical decisions. Their thrust is on as much objectivity as possible with personal preference only playing a limited part. The difficulty is that sometimes it is not possible or appropriate to systemise decision making in the way advocated in the book. But the eight keys above provide a helpful starting point.

Conclusion

Time spent observing good decision makers and learning from them is never wasted. Key questions to ask yourself might be:

- What have I learned from a good decision maker I have observed recently?
- How do others balance clarity and conviction?
- When does courage become foolhardy behaviour?
- What elements seem to be most important in the way hard decisions are communicated?

3

The Role of Christian Discernment

When faced with hard decisions two key questions to ask ourselves are:

- What are the sources of authority for our decisions?
- Are there Christian values that provide a basis for making hard decisions in particular circumstances?

'Sources of authority' and 'Christian values' are two overlapping issues in decision making. Sources of authority include God's purposes as expressed in creation, the life and work of Jesus, the ongoing work of the Holy Spirit, biblical insight, the lives of God's people and the accumulated experience of the Christian church and Christian leaders. Such sources of authority have to be seen in the current context. This does not undermine the sources of authority but means that they are looked at by each generation as it searches to apply eternal truth in the most relevant way.

Christian values provide a way perspective that can bring a freshness to how others might look at difficult decisions. The writer of the epistle to the Galatians talks of the fruits of the spirit as 'love, joy, peace, patience, kindness, goodness, faithfulness, gentleness and self-control' (Gal. 5:22). How do these characteristics impact the way we make decisions? In the same passage the writer to the Galatians talks of characteristics we should not embody, namely, 'becoming conceited, provoking and envying each other' (Gal. 5:26). Alongside these expressions of Christian living are the themes of compassion, forgiveness, new birth and hope which are central to the Gospel narratives. In his first epistle the apostle Peter talks of leaders being eager to serve and not lording it over those entrusted to them (1 Pet. 5:3).

It would be convenient if these themes from the Christian Gospel provided a definitive answer in any difficult situation. The reality is they provide a vital perspective but the individual or group is required to work out the right answer in a particular context.

For example, a willingness to forgive is central to the Christian perspective on human failure. But such forgiveness has to be tempered by compassion for those who have suffered because of a particular individual's action and those who might suffer from future actions by the individual. We will forever be balancing forgiveness for individuals and compassion for those affected more widely: decisions will involve 'winners and losers', and potentially those who will feel vindicated and those who will feel aggrieved.

The Christian facing a difficult decision seeks to reach an answer that is true to their Christian values. The answer may not be clear immediately. There may well be a process of 'seeing through a glass darkly' (1 Cor. 13:12).

What Is Distinctive about Christian Discernment?

In one sense the Christian has the same inputs as any reflective person: they have insights that come from physical, emotional or intellectual awareness. The Christian can and should listen clearly to views expressed to them. We have eyes, ears, experiences and intellectual and emotional understanding that provide crucial input. Is there a danger that we put seeking God's will as something separate from using our God-given gifts of understanding to find a way forward?

What is distinctive about Christian discernment is the richness of Christian experience, prayer, meditation and the clarity of understanding that can come through thinking through the teaching and approach of Jesus. There may be moments of complete clarity when there is a strong sense of being aligned with God's will. On other occasions it is much less clear cut, but there grows a quiet sense of being at peace with a particular decision when we sense that we are part of God's purposes in moving an issue to resolution.

Central to this is listening and listening again to each other and to all those with a perspective. The hard work of discernment is not about blanking out the views of those with whom we disagree. It is about working through hard questions, engaging fully and moving step-by-step to a resolution.

When I led a weekend on leadership with curates in a UK Midlands Anglican Diocese we talked about what helped them most in terms of discernment when a hard decision had to be made. Their main ways of working through discernment were:

- common sense and reason: applying the understanding that God had given them;
- trying to see the situation from God's perspective;
- building in strategic prayer, alone and with others;
- ensuring prayer is a central part of their lifestyle;

- bringing together both personal prayer, prayer in small groups and community prayer;
- drawing on the complementary gifts of others so that there is a sharing of perspective;
- encouraging honest feedback from others about the merits of different options;
- having a wise counselor with whom you can talk about any aspect of a problem;
- drawing on the advice of friends who become like 'guardian angels';
- standing back and making space to think through problems from a range of different angles;
- testing out a potential way forward in discussion with a range of different people and praying it through with friends; and
- taking some practical steps in a certain direction and then seeing what the reaction is and what your understanding is before making a final decision.

When I posed the same question with a group of leaders in Vancouver some of their comments were:

- ensure you have a clearly thought through framework in advance;
- be very conscious of the cultural influences so that you are not forced into a particular mould;
- ensure there is enough time to stand back and pray;
- for major decisions ensure there is an opportunity to go on retreat;
- bring in outsiders who can contribute different perspectives and insights including outsiders who may not share a Christian perspective but are sympathetic to what you are trying to do;

- keep this decision in perspective alongside other decisions;
- let a specific group do the hard work of thinking and working through next steps;
- think about how the different options might be consistent with the kingdom of God; and
- lay out the alternatives and narrow down the options before reflecting and praying about them.

It can be helpful to look at the perspective of respected theologians. I draw below from the perspectives of Bruce Waltke; J. I. Packer and Carolyn Nystrom; and Gordon Smith.

Bruce Waltke

In his book *Finding the Will of God: A Pagan Notion?* Bruce Waltke examines practices that Christians often describe as divine guidance, such as drawing lots and looking for signs. He suggests that the truest course to find the will of God is found instead in faithfully answering the call to walk close to God and be conformed to his likeness. He comments:

> My following of God is based upon my relationship with Him rather than on a special 'sign'. Rather than looking for some sort of wrapped spiritual package from the Almighty, I want to rely upon my closeness to Him. So when I wonder about which job offer to take, I don't go through a divination process to discover the hidden message of God. Instead I examine how God has called me to live my life, what my motives are, what He has given me a heart for, where I am in my walk with Christ, and what God is saying to me through His word and His people.

Countless times I have heard people quote Proverbs
3:5–6 as a basis for divining God's will: 'Trust in the
Lord with all thine heart, and lean not unto thine own
understand. In all thy ways acknowledge him, and he
shall direct thy paths' (KJV). Many people read the
word 'direct' and assume that this verse means God will
give them special direction in everyday decisions of life.
But the Hebrew word literally means to 'go straight' so
a sound exegesis reveals that if you trust God you will
not go outside the bounds of what the book of Proverbs
teaches. When it says that 'he shall direct thy paths' it
does not mean that God will offer you special revelation,
but that He will make your track right because you are
living your life in accordance with the words of Proverbs.
Using a verse as a magic incantation does not mean that
God is obliged to hand you the answer to your problem.
This is simply not true to Christian experience. Receiving
a message from God is nearly always in conjunction with
having a loving heart towards God. The Spirit of God
in your life, together with the influence of the Word,
illuminates the thoughts of the Lord.

Waltke is clear that God expects us to use our own judgment. He suggests that God guides us through his Word, then
through our heartfelt desires, then through the wise counsel
of others and then our own circumstances. He says:

> At that point we must rely on our own sound judgment.
> It is possible to pray, read God's word, seek counsel and
> still not feel led by God. That's the time to rely on sound
> judgment. God gave each of us a brain and he expects
> us to put it to good use . . . . God expects us to use our
> decision-making capabilities to make choices.

Waltke writes about sound judgment being within the framework of faith. He emphasises five things to consider in particular when relying upon your own judgment:

- *make your decision in the light of Scripture*—do not negate anything in Scripture or resort to human logic in violation of the Bible;
- *make your decision in the light of your giftedness*—reflect on whether the ramifications of a decision match your gifts;
- *make your decisions according to your ability*—do not try to be what you are not: be deliberately conscious of your skills and limitations;
- *make your decision according to your circumstances*—e.g., for Paul, many of his decisions were based on sound judgment rather than God giving miraculous answers; and
- *make your decision according to an overall strategy*—this provides a context for making long term decisions.

Waltke believes in a God who can perform miracles but does not find that miracles are the normal course of events for Christian direction. He suggest that 'laying out of the fleece' is generally the lazy person's way to discern the will of God as it requires no work, little discipline and almost no character development. He comments,

> The apostles never put out the equivalent of a fleece. Moreover, they never even hinted that Christians should look for 'signs' as a means of determining God's will. We should look for signs signalling the end of the age, but that is not the same thing as using signs for 'finding God's will'. Remember that Jesus promised that the

Comforter or Helper, the Holy Spirit, would teach the apostles all things and bring to their remembrance all the things that He had said to them (John 14:26). Jesus never taught His church to use signs in the way Gideon did. The Spirit enlightens (Eph. 1:17–18), regenerates (John 3:5–8), sanctifies (Gal. 5:16–18), transforms (2 Cor. 3:18; Gal. 5:22–23) and gives God's people what they need in order to serve Him (1 Cor. 12:4–11). God leads his people not through signs but through His Word, His Holy Spirit, His Church, Christian friends who offer godly counsel, and His providential circumstances. One of the lessons from the life of Jesus is that people will not turn to God simply because they see a miracle. Instead, they will simply ask for another miracle. So God leaves the miraculous for those few great moments when a miracle is the best way to alter the course of history.

J. I. Packer and Carolyn Nystrom

In their book *Guard Us, Guide Us: Divine Leading in Life's Decisions* J. I. Packer and Carolyn Nystrom refer to the fact that for many, discerning God's will has become fraught with fear and confusion. The authors have no time for any version of fortune telling (the appeal to arbitrary signs and humanly designed 'fleeces' to tell us what to do); nor for primary reliance on something best termed 'feeling-itis' (the appeal to strong feelings and hunches, however sudden and sustained, to tell us what to do). The authors suggest that discernment comes through listening to Scripture as alternatives are judged and as 'we wait on God, laying before him all the aspects of, and angles on, perplexing situations as we see them and asking for help to discern the proper path'.

The authors write of adult human life being a compound of three things: discovery, direction setting, and decision making with all three involving some form of relating, communicating, imagining and hoping. For them,

- *discovering* means the discerning of goodness, truth and beauty or their opposites in the world order that surrounds us and in our relationships with other people;
- *direction setting* means fixing personal goals and embracing purposeful action; and
- *decision making* means the establishing of our various commitments major and minor, some involving change, some confirming continuance, some following our usual habits, some breaking with them, and all being a positive responsive to whomever or whatever is confronting us each moment.

The authors write about being guided by the mind of God. They write of messy situations where there are no ideal answers but whatever is done has sad side effects and some disagreeable risks or consequences. They suggest,

> What is required of us in such messes is not to go hunting for Bible texts that speak directly to our circumstances (there are not likely to be any), but we are to practise prayerfully the art of applicatory thinking, using logic before the Lord to determine by the light of biblical principles the course that promises the most good and the least evil . . . it is always the best decision that circumstances allow that expresses the mind of God.

They reflect on the importance of role models on the basis that

- role models will enlarge our vision and help us to grasp more clearly the moral and spiritual ideals which have been held in high regard among Christians;
- role models can make us realise what should and could be in our lives, which is about demonstrating higher and better possibilities; and
- encountering a role model can also help vocationally, suggesting goals that we would not have imagined had we been left to ourselves.

The authors are clear that when seeking guidance we should always start by asking to be delivered from stupidity, pride and bigheadedness, and all forms of motivational perversity that would skew our thinking. We should ask for sensitivity, pure heartedness and clarity to discern what course of action will bring about the most good and honour God most fully. They see this line of prayer needing to be constantly churning in our hearts as we do the reading, thinking, talking and listening that our quest for discernment requires of us.

Gordon T. Smith

In his book *The Voice of Jesus: Discernment, Prayer and the Witness of the Spirit* Gordon Smith describes the word *discernment* as implying three different concepts simultaneously:

- first, it includes the idea of *insight*, which speaks of the capacity to see something clearly;
- second, it includes the idea of *discretion*, the capacity to distinguish between good and evil as well as between the good and the better; and
- third, it includes the idea of *judgment*: a judgment that is informed by knowledge and understanding.

He sees the ability to discern the voice of Jesus as a crucial spiritual skill, basic to the capacity to make vocational and moral choices.

> Discernment is learnt over time, as we come to recognise the movements of God in our hearts. We discover that we must learn to trust our emotions and our inner intuition while simultaneously acknowledging our capacity for self deception. Discernment calls us to attend to the heart in a way that is informed by our critical faculties so that we are not easily misled.

Smith refers to the description of the Holy Spirit as the 'Spirit of Truth' which suggests a distinctive and important relationship between the Spirit and Truth. He suggests,

> We only listen, only attend to the Spirit when we come with open hearts and open hands before the Truth: this is the posture of life giving humility, the disposition that enables us to truly engage the Spirit of the Living God.

He describes choosing well as an art, but first it is a burden that has to be accepted:

> We cannot choose well unless we first, willingly and without bitterness, accept the reality that choices are a part of life and that we will not live in truth and freedom unless we act. Sometimes this means that we accept the reality of a Y in the road, a decision that is forced upon us. We can resent this or gracefully accept it as part of life. We cannot grow in both directions. Sometimes our choosing is a matter of courage . . . we choose as an act of life and as an intentional response to the call of God on our lives.

He continues:

> Our decision making is our responsibility. It is our act
> of choosing in response to the options, problems and
> opportunities that are placed before us. God does not
> choose for us, and we cannot expect others to make our
> choices for us, not if we want to accept adult responsibil-
> ity for our lives. Indeed, the capacity to discern well and
> make wise decisions is a crucial sign of spiritual maturity
> . . . . God is good and gracious and often keeps us from
> experiencing the full consequences of foolish decisions
> but there is no excuse for not learning to decide well.

He suggests that we should each be able to speak with
clarity in response to the question, "How do you make decisions?" There should be, for each of us, a self-conscious awareness of how we work our way through the choices that will
inevitably come our way. He says that although we speak of
decision making in the same breath as discernment, and even
though we recognise the presence of the Spirit of God in our
choosing, this act is never so mysterious that we cannot speak
with clarity about how we make decisions.

He writes of effective decision making and discernment
requiring the engagement of both heart and mind:

> Discernment requires attentiveness to what we see and
> observe as well as to what is happening to us emotion-
> ally. Our capacity to discern is not merely a matter of
> rational analysis of our environment and of the strengths
> and limitations on a particular situation: it is also an in-
> tuitive response that is informed by our encounter with
> Christ and by our own emotional response to the world
> and Christ.

Smith talks of nurturing a receptivity to God through the discipline of prayer. He suggests that God does not merely give us wisdom but through his personal presence in our lives enables us to grow in wisdom—a wisdom that is formed through personal encounter.

Smith says that part of knowing ourselves is realising what causes our tendency towards procrastination. He suggests that many Christians are happy to relinquish their adult responsibility and remain in a posture of spiritual dependence on another rather than cultivating their own capacity for discernment.

Perspectives from Current Leaders

For those in leadership roles discernment has to be seen in a very practical light. Below are a few perspectives from individuals in influential roles.

Stephen Bampfylde, the managing director of the leading UK headhunting firm Saxton Bampfylde Hever, talks of addressing decisions in the following way:

> Make them slowly. If it is possible never make a decision on the day it is first presented to you. Park it. Pray about it and see what you think in the morning. God works through our unconscious mind as well as our conscious mind. If after reflection the decision seems right it is likely to be in accordance with my values and the firm's values.

Alastair Redfern, the bishop of Derby, suggests the following perspective about discernment when making difficult decisions:

You pray about it. You seek a sense of God's guidance. You look at the whole picture together. Prayer is when you step back into God's space. You reflect on what the Christian Gospel is saying today. You take care against closing down decisions to one dimension. Sometimes you have to carry the pain for people. Sometimes you have to recognise that you cannot win, this is a key part to keeping it in perspective. You are conscious about ambiguity, but as a Christian leader you bring clarity. You have to give clarity to others weighing up different considerations.

You must be sensitive to all the information you hear. You need to be able to see the situation from the perspective of other people. You recognise that forgiveness is important but so is tough love. Discernment may be about bringing into account the context of the wider church and the Gospel's reputation. You have to handle situations from the perspective not only of the individual but from the perspective of the wider church and the Gospel.

Matt Baggott is the Chief Constable of Leicestershire Police Constabulary in the UK. His approach when faced with a hard decisions is:

> I try to reflect on what needs to be resolved. I try to find time to put it before the Lord. It is important I do not close off the Holy Spirit. As a professional I get the right team round the table and I encourage honesty and plainly speaking. I am conscious of my own frailty. I trust that the Lord lives within me and that I won't hang onto things that will deflect me.

Judy Hirst, the Director of Collaborative Ministry in the Durham and Newcastle Dioceses in the UK and author of

Struggling to be Holy reflects on Christian discernment within decision making:

> It is very difficult to discern your motivation. For me the guiding principle is what is loving rather than selfish or destructive. It is not just what I want to do. It is about applying Christian values and assumptions. It is about being clear on what is important, wanting to be aligned with God's will and living out God's will in particular situations.
>
> It is about being honest with God, telling him what you think and what is difficult, and then trusting God for peace. It is being open about complexity and all you think and feel. It is accepting shared decisions. It is always coming back to what is the loving thing to do in this situation.

In these examples there is a balance between:

- the need to reflect before making a decision;
- the importance of being professional while listening to your conscious mind; and
- allowing prayer and prayerfulness to be part of decisions in a secular context.

Sometimes bad decisions make for very successful outcomes and are celebrated as good decisions. Conversely, good decisions can split the team, throw the enterprise into confusion, generate extreme hostility and lead to your own demise: Jesus' journey to the cross would be a classic example. Good decisions need to have a fundamental moral integrity before God, not just outputs that please people and seem successful to our eyes.

Conclusion

What I hope these examples have done is to demystify discernment. We cannot know the fully workings of the Holy Spirit, but we can approach seeking discernment in a rational and purposeful way, seeking to look through the eyes of Jesus and being open to both the facts and insights which flow from our engagement with the Spirit of the Living God.

Questions to ask yourself might be:

- What do you think is distinctive about Christian discernment when approaching hard decisions?
- How helpful is the suggestion from Bruce Waltke that the truest way to find the will of God is found in faithfully answering the call to walk close to God and be conformed to his likeness?
- How might you react if someone plays the 'God card' and insists their approach is the only valid one?

4

What Is Your Approach
to Decision Making?

Each of us has a way of making or not making hard decisions. The approach we tend to adopt results from the way we are made, our cultural background and our mix of experiences. Each of us has a framework we use whether we like it or not. Should we ever modify that framework? Our experience of life and living our faith may tell us that our current approach to making hard decisions is generally fine, or is flawed or random.

Self-awareness is helpful in understanding the way we make difficult decisions. Some of us are reflective and will need longer than others to reach a decision. Some of us will know what we think about a particular issue when we hear ourselves articulate it. Becoming better at making hard decisions is not about each of us using the same approach. Our understanding of ourselves, the context in which we live and our faith will mean we may well use different approaches. Perhaps the most important element is that we decide consciously what approach we are going to take to making hard decisions.

Your Own Framework

Can I encourage you to think about your own framework for making hard decisions which builds on a self-awareness of yourself, incorporates your Christian understanding and values, builds on your own experience of decision making and is relevant to the type of decisions you will be making in the future? Then can I encourage you to test out your approach with trusted others so that your approach is both personal and draws from the Christian understanding and wisdom of those you trust? Try it out and be willing to learn what works well and what does not!

One approach is to use the framework set out earlier: seeking a balance between clarity and conviction and adapting that approach to meet your circumstances. It may mean defining:

- what elements of clarity are most important to you (e.g., the appropriate facts, analysis and objective data); and
- what aspects of conviction are relevant in this situation (e.g., your values, intuition, trained judgment and experience).

An important part of developing our ability to make hard decisions is learning from experience. Sometimes we can be captured by guilt or regret if a decision goes wrong. We need to be released from our own debilitating captivity by allowing ourselves to move on and learn from our mistakes. A vicar I knew when I was an undergraduate had on his wall a plaque saying 'Hallelujah Anyway', which acted as a reminder of the importance of giving thanks in any situation. Key questions to ask ourselves when we regret a decision might be:

- Why did I make the original decision?
- What good has flowed from the decision?
- Why do I regret the decision?
- How can I best move on from this situation?
- How do I embed my learning from this situation?

Changing Attitudes

When I was challenged recently about what was the hardest decision I had had to make, my instinctive response was that the hardest decisions were about changing my perspective or attitude. They were about changing deep rooted assumptions about success and failure, about what is Christian ambition and what is Christian service. The difficult decisions were about turning to face a different direction in terms of what is success and what is Christian servanthood.

Perhaps one way of developing a new way of looking at hard decisions is not just to look at the decision itself, but also to look at the perspective or mindset we bring to the decision. Might there be rigidities within our mindset that make a decision more difficult than it should be? If we are too fixated on what personal success is, some decisions may be either very difficult or depressing. If we can look afresh at our initial mindset, allowing it to be reframed through reflection, meditation, reflection and prayer, we may find we come fresh to revisit hard decisions. A career decision, for example, may become much easier having worked through anew what Christian service and vocation means.

As you reflect on your own approach to decision making, I invite you to reflect on perspectives from Henri Nouwen, C. S. Lewis, Peter Ducker and Bob Buford.

Choose Your Attitude

Henri Nouwen is clear that we can choose our own attitudes. In *Bread for the Journey* he writes,

> Choices make the difference. Two people are in the same accident, one is severely wounded. They did not choose to be in the accident. It happened to them. But one of them chose to live the experience in bitterness, the other in gratitude. These choices radically influence their lives and the lives of their families and friends. We have very little control over what happens in our lives, but we have a lot of control over how we integrate and remember what happens. It is precisely these spiritual choices that determine whether we live our lives with dignity.

Nouwen quotes Deuteronomy 30:19, which says, 'I am offering you life or death, blessing or curse. Choose life, then, so you and your descendants may live'. From this he emphasises the importance of our underlying attitude and approach:

> 'Choose life,' that's God's call for us, and there is not a moment in which we do not have to make that choice. Life and death are always before us. In our imaginations, our thoughts, our words, our gestures, our actions . . . even in our non-actions. This choice for life starts in a very interior place. Underneath very life-affirming behaviour I can still harbour death-thoughts and death-feelings. The most important question is not 'Do I kill'? but 'Do I carry a blessing in my heart or a curse'? The bullet that kills is only the final instrument of hatred that began in the heart long before the gun was picked up.

Seek God's Heart

In his book *In the Name of Jesus: Reflections on Christian Leadership* Nouwen writes of asking himself, 'What decisions have you been making lately and how are they a reflection of the way you sense the future'? He says that sometimes, 'I have to trust that God is at work in me and that the way I am being moved to new inner and outer places is part of a larger movement of which I am only a very small part'. He emphasises the importance of seeking to know the heart of God as it has become flesh, 'a heart of flesh' in Jesus. He writes,

> Knowing God's heart means consistently, radically and very concretely to announce and reveal that God is love and only love, and that every time fear, isolation, and despair begins to invade the human cell this is not something that comes from God. This sounds very simple and maybe trite, but very few people know that they are loved without any conditions or limits.

Understand the Implications of Your Choices

In *Mere Christianity* C. S. Lewis writes about the importance each choice has on who we are. He comments,

> Every time you make a choice you are turning the central part of you, the part of you that chooses, into something a little different from what is was before. And taking your life as a whole, with all your innumerable choices, all your life long you are slowly turning this central thing either into a heavenly creature or into a hellish creature: either into a creature that is in harmony with God, and with other creatures, and with itself, or else into one that is in a state of war and hatred with God, and with its fellow creatures, and with itself. To be the one kind of

creature is heaven: that is, it is joy and peace and knowledge and power. To be the other means madness, horror,
idiocy, rage, impotence and eternal loneliness. Each of
us at each moment is progressing to either one state or
the other.

Lewis uses the graphic description that as we make choices we are turning ourselves into either heavenly creatures or
hellish creatures. This is as much about how we make decisions as the decisions themselves because of the effect we can
easily have on others as we reflect or agonise over decisions.

See Making Choices as an Opportunity

In his foreword to Bob Buford's book *Stuck at Half-time* Peter
Ducker writes of the increased opportunity to make choices:

> In a few hundred years when the history of our time is
> written from a long term perspective I think it is very
> probable that the most important event those histori-
> ans will remember is not technology, not the Internet,
> not e-commerce but the unprecedented change in the
> human condition. For the first time—and I mean that
> literally—substantial and rapidly growing numbers of
> people have choices. For the first time people have to
> manage themselves.

In this book Buford talks of lives limited by our own re-
stricting choices:

> A life limited by our own choices is a tragic life that
> will never become what God fully intended. We were
> created to make a difference, to leave something behind
> of meaning. At no time in history have we had such op-
> portunity to enjoy life to its fullest in ways that bring

happiness and fulfilment to ourselves and betterment for those who need it.

His message is that our opportunity to make choices is often growing, whatever the constraints we see around. We can either focus on the factors limiting our scope to make decisions, or we can see the opportunity to make choices as a welcome responsibility. We certainly have the opportunity to chose our attitude!

Conclusion

Key questions to ask as you reflect on the way you make hard decisions are:

- What for you is the best way of balancing clarity and conviction?
- How can you best choose your attitude when you make decisions?
- How do you ensure that your Christian understanding impacts effectively as you make decisions?

5

Key Questions
in Making Decisions

This chapter looks at key issues that arise when making decisions using a sequence of questions. The questions addressed are:

- What is the role of external support such as consultancy, mentoring, coaching and spiritual direction?
- What is the role of shared leadership in making hard decisions?
- How might uncertainty be handled and measured risks taken that are not foolhardy?
- What are the particular difficulties involved in having a leadership role in both a secular job and a Christian world?
- How do you best cope in a situation where questions of truth become reduced to questions of power?
- How best do we live with ambiguity and imperfection when making hard decisions?
- How do we live with decisions whether they are right or wrong?

- How might you best prepare to make hard decisions?
- What might you do when your heart says one thing and your head says another?
- Where do compassion and fairness fit in to making hard decisions?
- How do we best live with the mixed motives which often underlie our decision making?
- How do you recover when decisions go wrong?
- What if financial pressures rule out a good decision?
- How can you draw effectively on the perspectives of others?
- What do you do when there is no clear answer?
- How do you best live with ambiguity and non-ideal options?

The Role of External Support

There is a danger that we try to tackle difficult decisions alone: the more difficult a decision the more we sometimes take the burden of it solely on our shoulders. External support can play a crucial part: it is not an admittance of weakness but an acknowledgement of the importance of having trusted external sources of input. There are few situations more dangerous than when an individual is allowed to get fixated on a particular angle and does not draw on external perspectives. Valuable sources of input can be:

- *consultancy*, from those with an expertise in a particular situation, e.g., they have managed or advised on change programmes before and have relevant experience that can help you make difficult decisions when

you are working through change in your organisation;

- *mentoring,* which is about discussions with a purpose
  with leaders who have themselves been through a
  similar situation and have personal experience that
  can be drawn on;

- *coaching,* where focused conversations with a coach
  who has experience from parallel situations in very
  different environments can enable you to reach new
  insights; and

- *spiritual direction,* where a wise Christian can bring
  insight from the richness of the biblical narrative or
  other Christian writers whose words bear particularly
  on your individual circumstances.

It will rarely be input from all four of these strands at the
same time; it will depend partly on what sources of support
are available at any particular time. Crucial to the growing
of wisdom in any Christian is the personal development that
comes through stretching and engaging relationships with
those who have been on the journey longer. For example, the
good coach will help somebody develop rigour in their thinking and then have the courage of their convictions to take a
hard decision through to conclusion.

The Role of Shared Leadership

Jesus did not make hard decisions alone; he prayed to his
Father. There was a sharing of a decision through his prayers,
even though as Son of God he was in a unique position. Shared
leadership has strong biblical roots; Jesus chose a group of
people to be his disciples. The apostles worked together as
a group in shaping the early church. When Paul went on

his journeys he took Barnabas and then Silas with him. The secular organisation that is well run will have a balance of responsibilities between Chair and Chief Executive, or between the Board and the senior management. Experience over the centuries has demonstrated the value within Christian organisations of having a balance of responsibility between the minister and the elders or between the vicar and the church wardens. Shared leadership is not about the abdication of responsibility but is about the importance of bringing together different perspectives where the overall leadership capacity is more than just the sum of the parts.

Very few hard decisions should be made alone. Even when the ultimate responsibility rests with one individual, talking a decision through with trusted others can provide both new insights and resolve. In any organisation the decision that is just dumped down by the leader is unlikely to engender commitment and energy. A shared commitment to outcomes is fundamental to success or else the pack of cards is likely to collapse. Effective shared leadership is all about understanding each other; trusting each other; learning together; encouraging each other; living with our differences and turning them to our advantage; and delivering outcomes together. In any organisation building a strong sense of shared participation in leadership provides the robustness and the capacity to cope with change. This is just as true in Christian organisations as in secular organisations.

Handling Uncertainty and Measuring Risks

There is a danger that the Christian leader might be so clear about the answer that they rush to specific conclusions, or they may be so sensitive to the views of others that they live in a world of complete indecision. How do we find an effective way through this dilemma? How can we ensure that our way of handling uncertainty is not to rush to an instant answer or to allow ourselves to wallow in a sea of indecision? It is partially about accepting that uncertainty will always be there. There will always be variables we cannot nail down. The rapidity of change will mean that as soon as we think we have clarity, some other factor will have put us in danger of falling back into confusion. Uncertainty, although annoying, has its virtues too: it will mean that we will be more open to surprises and more willing to accept that there may be fresh insights and new angles that are helpful and not just annoying. The Scriptures talk of the Spirit of God coming in unexpected ways. As Christians we should always be ready to recognise that when we are uncertain God may be speaking to us in different and new ways.

A few years ago risk assessment was something done by accountants. Now it is at the centre of any enterprise or project which is doing its job seriously. Risk assessment is not about finding reasons not to do things. It is about looking at the consequences of different possibilities and planning how to respond to different events. Robust risk assessment should be at the heart of the attempts of any organisation planning ahead to cope with uncertainty. Any change programme in a secular or Christian organisation will involve risks. Boldness will be important to ensure success, but looking at risks carefully and making contingent plans is part of using the gifts of intellect and reason that God has given to us.

Differences between Leading Christian and Secular Organizations

An individual who is making decisions in their secular employment will be used to a pattern of decision making that is appropriate to their area of work be it in a factory, school, office or hospital. There will be patterns of authority and values they are used to. As a Christian they will be interrelating their personal values to the organisational values and being an influence for good within that organisation.

Many of the same disciplines will transfer to the individual's work within a Christian organisation or church but the individual may need to adjust their approach. Within the secular organisation employees may be sharing a similar set of expectations and come from a similar background. Within the church there may be greater diversity of social background, age and education. Within a business context discussion and debate may be the norm, but for many people discussion and debate can be threatening and unsettling, and a different form of listening and engagement may be necessary. Decision making may take longer and need more iterations and different approaches until there is enough of a common mind to move on. The experiences of leadership in the secular world are likely to be very helpful but may well need to be tempered in the church or wider charity world by our compassion for others, a pragmatism about what will work within a voluntary organisation, and by a very different set of values and desired outcomes.

Truth and Power

In pressured situations questions of truth can become reduced to questions of power, where truth is wrapped up in half truth and bundled together with speculation that borders on the dishonest and deceitful. Timing can be critical where opinion is polarised, between strong and decisive early action as against patient courage under fire until you see 'the whites of the opponent's eyes'. Both can be presented as strength or weakness. The challenge for the Christian in these circumstances is to be clear about their values, discern what is truth and what is fabrication, offer thought through counsel, hold their nerve and see the immediate decision in a wider context of what is or is not important.

Ambiguity and Imperfection

Sometimes there is a clear right and a wrong answer. The husband who beats up his wife is in the wrong whatever the provocation, but many decisions are not as clear cut. The prison governor who is deciding whether to release a prisoner on temporary release has to make a judgement based partially on evidence and partially on his belief about whether an individual can be trusted. He cannot know precisely what will happen: possibly the prisoner whose release is being considered does not know himself what his behaviour will be like, however well intentioned he may feel at the moment. Whenever hard decisions are to be made there will be uncertainty about the outcome. The individual who is confirmed or admitted into church membership cannot guarantee their perfection. Just as we live with imperfections in ourselves so we have to live with imperfections in the way decisions are made.

Part of living with ambiguity and imperfection is reaching decisions for the best of reasons and then accepting that sometimes those decisions will prove right, and sometimes wrong. When a new leader or teacher is appointed there will be a careful weighing of the evidence and thinking through of the effects of an individual appointment, but there can be no guarantee of success. Living with ambiguity and imperfection is about making decisions responsibly and then accepting that it is often up to others to turn that decision into a successful outcome. If the outcome is not as intended we have the peace that the decision was made for the best of reasons based on the best of evidence.

Living with Decisions

Some decisions have to be made instantaneously. But for many decisions there can be a time of standing back before the final decision point. It is that moment of careful reflection that can help us live with the outcome of the decisions then made. The Christian focus of forgiveness is central to living with decisions whether they are right or wrong. The Christian has the belief that when decisions are made for the best of reasons there can be forgiveness if they are wrong. That is no reason to legitimise foolhardy decisions, but it does help that the Christian believes that they can be forgiven for a wrong decision; although it often means they need to seek the forgiveness of their colleagues and family, as well as seeking the forgiveness of God through prayer.

Effective Preparation

This will vary by individual but might include writing out the pros and cons of a particular decision, talking it through with trusted friends, using a structured type of prayer, creating space to think about the issue from different angles which might come through walking, running, listening to music or creating reflecting space on one's own.

Head versus Heart

A first step might be being honest with yourself in describing the ambivalent reactions you are experiencing. It is being as clear as possible about why your head is saying one thing and your heart another. How much is this based on an objective understanding of what is happening, or how much are you being influenced by a rather rigid thought process or by the emotional reaction that comes from a dominant previous experience or a sense of vulnerability? Reconciling heart and head might be helped by asking some 'what if' questions to see which variables are giving you most concern. Maybe your heart and head will never come entirely into line, but talking the different perspectives through with friends might help with understanding why there is a difference between them and then enable you to reach a way forward with which you are more comfortable. Sometimes God may be speaking to you particularly through your heart and at other times through your head.

Compassion and Fairness

Some of the most difficult decisions involve balancing compassion to one individual and fairness to others. How often do you forgive somebody who has not been doing their job well? You want to give them every opportunity to succeed, but their failings may be having a detrimental effect on others with resentment growing because you have not dealt firmly with this situation. Perhaps the answer is to try and build more of a shared understanding among all those affected. It might be sharing your belief that personal development and change is possible and to be encouraging, while making clear that the principle of 'loving your neighbour as yourself' does mean balancing showing compassion to one individual and fairness to others, recognising that each member of a team needs to play a part if somebody's performance is going to rise to a higher level.

Mixed Motives

However we present our motives there can sometimes be an underlying ambition or envy that can influence our approach to decisions. We like to be proved right and therefore objectivity may not always be at its strongest. We need the humility to accept that our perspective may not be as balanced as we would like, the humility to be honest about what might be the balance of motives influencing us, and the holiness to allow our 'best character' to be uppermost in the way we make our decisions.

Recovering from Bad Decisions

There will be times when one decision after another has gone 'pear shaped'. You feel let down either by others or by yourself. But like the jockey thrown off the horse, it is a matter of getting up and getting back in the saddle and then perhaps not making the same mistake again!

Two dangers when decisions go wrong are blaming either God or ourselves. Any hint of blaming God for our decisions that go wrong is a dangerous sign that we might be on a path leading to resentment which will inhibit our ability to make decisions in the future. Acknowledging our part in making a wrong decision is one thing, but blaming ourselves when we have thought about an issue carefully is neither fair to ourselves nor helpful to others if we are to be able to make effective decisions again in the future.

Financial Pressures

Christian leadership is a combination of a boldness of vision alongside an acceptance of practical reality. There are times when we step out in faith with an adventurous plan and seek the resources to go with it. If the resources follow we regard God as blessing us. If the resources do not, we can become depressed and down-hearted and think that God in some way does not regard us as worthy. But it might have been the right idea at the wrong time. It might be that through the experience of the financial resources not being there, our faith and the way we think about what is possible is being moulded, not just by reality but by God, who is continually shaping our thinking through the experience of faith and life.

Drawing Effectively on the Perspective of Others

The right answer will depend on the particular context, but the principle about the importance of drawing on the perspective of others is crucial to hold on to. It may be at more than one level. It can include informal networks which allow a greater understanding to be built up; it may also involve formal accountability structures with groups remitted to take forward action in particular areas. Drawing on trusted others can be about sharing the load emotionally (through the support of friends), spiritually (through the prayer of others) and formally (through structures that bring together different sources of expertise).

Talking an issue through with a mentor or coach can be very helpful, but some decisions remain clearly yours: the value of such discussions is to help strengthen the quality of your reflection and analysis, but it is not sharing the decision itself!

When There Is No Clear Answer

It could mean waiting until the answer becomes clearer. It might mean parking a decision for a while or waiting for new information or insights. It might mean looking at that same situation from a variety of different angles and perspectives over time. Sometimes a decision has to be made when there might be no right or wrong answer; it might mean a trial period or some other way of testing out an option. When there appears to be no right answer it can be a matter of making an initial decision in your mind, then seeing what your own reactions are to that 'decision' and then reflecting on whether you feel peaceful about it as you talk through the consequences with others in quiet moments of reflection and prayer.

The experience of so many people when making decisions has been, 'If in doubt, don't'. Most decisions can be put off for a while to see if further perspectives are available. The ability to wait and watch in a faster world may mean holding your nerve when others are urging you to decide or to change your view. The period of reflection is rarely wasted.

Living with Both Ambiguity and Non-Ideal Options

We want life to be straightforward and unambiguous. Living with ambiguity seems like second best, but we have to live with contradictions in ourselves and others. When we make decisions there will always be mixed reactions; we will never be able to predict the full consequences of our actions. The reality is we have little option but to reconcile ourselves to living with some ambiguity, while at the same time bringing as much clarity as we can in the way any decision is addressed and taken forward.

Conclusion

When faced with a decision a good starting point is to identify the key questions about the issue and reflect on how you are going to respond to them. The questions might be about how you are going to handle your own apprehension and fears. As you look honestly at your fears it enables you to bring to bear your insights that come from the range of your experience alongside your intellectual, emotional and spiritual understanding. What is particularly important is how your responses are informed by your Christian values and character.

6

Addressing Specific Decisions

For the Christian leader, either in Christian organisations or in the secular world, hard decisions might be about strategic priorities, short term priorities, the use of time and energy, management issues, and choices about next steps. This chapter looks at each of these in turn, identifies a sequence of key questions for reflection and prayer, and sets out some illustrative examples as a basis for reflection.

Strategic Priorities

What should be the long term priorities of an organisation of which you are part? How do you balance practical reality with the desire to bring the presence of God into a particular area or sector? Key questions might be:

- What are the strategic opportunities that are opening up?
- What are the constraints that cannot be ignored?
- What would success look like five years from now?
- What are the actions that will make the biggest impact over the next five years?

- What is the relevance of Christian themes like creation, compassion, hope, new birth and resurrection?
- What in the long term might be the impact that Christian values might have in this evolving situation?

Roger had a major decision to make as a Chief Executive: should he go for a big expansion of the business or keep the business steady? He spent time reflecting on the following questions:

- Why did I see expansion as a good thing?
- Where does personal ambition fit in; is it getting in the way?
- What is the expert advice on whether expansion would be right?
- Do the staff and stakeholders want to see expansion?
- What will expansion do to the quality of lives of the employees?
- Are there ways in which expansion could lead to greater positive influence in the local community?
- Is the required extra marketing of the products we produce going to be consistent with my values?
- How will I balance my extra time commitment with my other personal responsibilities?
- Will the overall effect on customers and staff be positive in terms of having an effect for good in the world?

The result of discussion with trusted others and quiet reflection and prayer was Roger deciding to hold back from large scale expansion because of uncertainties in the market and the effect that the work involved in striving for a big expansion would have on himself, his family and his staff. Instead he decided to focus on expanding in some specific areas where he felt the business could bring the biggest benefit to the quality of individual lives. On reflection he was content that the decision both took account of economic realities and was rooted in his personal values about the well being of his staff and customers.

Short Term Priorities

This is often about balancing different interests or using human and financial resources to best effect. Is there scope to bring a Christian perspective that is both eternally valid and cognisant of practical reality? Key questions might be:

- What are the outcomes that would flow from different options?
- How does a Christian perspective influence the way I look at the priorities?
- How will different priorities impact different people or groups of people?
- Can I sit inside the consequences of different possibilities so I can see them more clearly?
- How will different priorities impact the reputation of the organisation and the values it stands for?
- How can those adversely affected by decisions be supported and cared for?

Stella was deciding whether to create another deputy head post in the school where she was head teacher. She was balancing a range of pressures for additional resources. Would it look selfish if she appointed a new deputy to ease the burdens on her? The steps Stella took were to listen carefully to different views and to put together a proposition that set out honestly the pros and cons. She encouraged independent people to give their feedback on the proposition. Stella began to imagine having made the decision and assessed her own reactions. She set aside a couple of hours one weekend to reflect and pray about the decision and to listen to her heart to see which way it was taking her. She reflected on how she would use the extra time that would now be available to her. When she made the decision she committed it explicitly before God in prayer trusting that she had made the right decision.

The Use of Time and Energy

Time may be a finite commodity but energy is, to an extent, variable. Key issues in decision making relate to the effective use of time and the way we harness energy to the best possible effect. Key questions about the use of your own time and energy might be:

- How self-aware am I about when I use time well and when I use it badly?
- How best do I create time to reflect and be strategic?
- Can I use times of preparation better so that time with people is used more productively?
- How can I best develop the way I use times of reading Scripture and of prayer so that I am more open to listening and reflecting?
- Do I fully recognize the sources of vitality that come from conversation, meditation, prayer, worship and engagement with the wider world?

Bill wanted to be promoted to the next grade in his job, to spend more time with his family and to do more at church.

A couple of friends wisely said to him that he would have to choose where he put his time and energy. Bill was taken aback by the frankness of the comments from his friends, but decided he must reflect and pray. What he did was seek the views of his wife on what was most important to her. He reflected on why he wanted to be promoted and how much time and energy he was willing to commit to work. He thought about where he could add most value at work and how he could focus his energy to maximum effect. He reflected on where he could make the most effective contribution at church and complement the input of others. He allowed himself to reflect on how his God given gifts might be developed and used for the benefit of others. He spent time praying and reflecting on his own and spent time in prayer with trusted others, allowing God to speak through both his mind and his heart.

Eventually he was at peace with a way forward and had greater clarity about his relative priorities within work, family and church. He knew it would be a delicate balance, but he felt he had moved to a point where he was making a conscious and not a haphazard set of decisions.

Management Issues

Christian leaders are not exempt from management responsibilities for people and resources. Too often the assertion that 'God will sort it out' is an abdication of responsibility. Key questions might be:

- Am I completely clear about the management responsibilities that fall to me?
- Am I clear about how different responsibilities sit alongside each other, e.g., legal responsibilities and accountabilities to different people?

- Do I have the best possible sources of advice and support?
- Am I accepting of the way my Christian values interrelate with my management responsibilities?
- Is there a shared understanding between myself and those for whom I have a 'duty of care' about respective responsibilities?
- Am I willing to make hard decisions which affect an individual's future if that becomes necessary?
- Could I explain openly to the risen Christ why I made a particular decision and not be embarrassed about it?

Helen had a tough decision to make. Should she dismiss a member of staff or give him another chance? The staff member had been fiddling his flextime and been found out. Some staff were sympathetic because of his personal circumstances; others thought he should be firmly disciplined. The action Helen took was as follows. She ensured that there was no ambiguity about the facts, and followed the organisation's normal disciplinary proceedings meticulously. She made sure she understood what the perspectives of other staff were. She put her crossness on one side to try to ensure she understood why the individual had taken the action he did. She tried to understand how deep the individual's remorse was and how likely he was to fiddle the system again. Helen was meticulous in understanding what were the boundaries of her discretion.

Helen prayed about the decision and committed it before God, allowing some time before she reached a final decision. She then set out some provisional conclusions and shared them with trusted others, and she tested her conclusions against the facts and her values.

The decision was between downgrading or dismissing. She reflected on what was the right balance between fairness to everyone else in the organisation and compassion to the individual. In this case she decided to downgrade and not dismiss because she believed that he had learnt his lesson. When giving the individual this news she recognised that how she gave the message was important. She was firm and kind, allowing the individual to come to terms with the outcome. She had upheld this individual in prayer throughout the process and continued to do so after the event.

Choices about Next Steps

Some of the hardest decisions are about our own next steps that will have ramifications for other people. We may be torn between doing what we think is right and the expectations of others. There may be a sense of duty that weighs heavily upon us. Key questions might be:

- What advice about next steps am I receiving from those I trust?
- What avenues do my head or heart think I should explore?
- What would give me the greatest sense of fulfilment?
- Where could I make the biggest contribution in terms of service to others?
- Do I feel any sense of 'calling' which is endorsed by people I trust?

At the heart of making progress in each of these areas is asking yourself questions which enable you to interrelate your human and Christian understanding. Hopefully the questions above provide a useful focus for working through next steps.

Ellen was wrestling with next steps in her life. Should she stay in her job or move into work with a church? She felt under pressure to take forward Christian service, but was not at peace with such a commitment. The actions Ellen took were to seek feedback on her strengths and areas for development. She talked through different options with trusted friends and her mentor. She projected her thinking a few years ahead, imagining what sort of contribution would give her most joy and fulfilment. Ellen saw opportunities to live out her Christian values and commitment in both option, but in different spheres. She reflected on what difference she, as a Christian, could make in these two different spheres. She spent some time in quiet retreat reflecting on the different options and seeing what her level of anticipation or excitement was with respect to each option.

She was open to either direction. She decided to spend some time shadowing leaders in both her current work area and in the church world. Gradually there was a strong sense of peace about staying for the moment in her current area of work, while taking forward training to become a lay minister in her church.

Conclusion

In all of these types of decisions the sequence of thinking and reflecting might helpfully follow a pattern of questions, such as:

- What are the facts?
- What is my starting point, based on my intellectual, emotional and Christian understanding?

- What are my values telling me?
- Are my emotional reactions distorting my perspective?
- When I reflect and pray what do I feel uneasy about?
- What are the fixed points for me which are consistent with my view of the facts and the key values that are relevant?
- What do I think is the right thing to do?
- How do I best triangulate with trusted others whether my judgment is securely based?
- Does the decision bring credit or discredit to the behaviours that Jesus espoused?
- Do I understand and accept the effect that the decision will have on others?

7

Increasing Your Capacity
to Make Hard Decisions

This chapter looks at practical steps for developing the capacity to make hard decisions. It looks first at developing the capacity in human terms and then at the dimension which comes from a Christian perspective. Ten points of good practice are identified in each section. There is inevitably and rightly an overlap between the two sections as Christians are making decisions in a secular world that God has created.

Developing Your Capacity to Make Hard Decisions: General Understanding and Skills

1. Observe others making decisions

Watching those who make decisions well can be very revealing. It may be worth noting down, after you have seen someone make a good decision with a constructive outcome, what they did well and share that perspective with a friend or colleague. In workshops I often invite people in pairs to identify generic characteristics of good decision makers. It is equally helpful to look at bad decisions or decision makers and crystallise the learning about what has gone wrong. The important step is then applying this learning to the way you make decisions!

2. Bring as much clarity as possible

This is about training yourself to be as objective as possible and being willing to base decisions on firm evidence, even when the evidence is contrary to what you had previously assumed. It is always asking questions about the facts, the information and the risks.

3. Understand your convictions

This is about understanding and applying your values, intuition and trained judgement. It is recognising that facts always have to be set in a wider context of values and beliefs. It is recognising your instinctive reaction, listening to it and building an understanding about when it is a reliable guide and when there is an emotional distortion that is embedded within it.

4. Build up self knowledge

The good decision maker understands their own strengths and weaknesses and is not caught in a spiral of self analysis. They know enough about themselves to interpret their own reactions and perspectives accurately. This self knowledge can come through personal reflection, feedback from others or psychometric assessments.

5. Learn from experience

Whether a decision has gone right or wrong there is always scope for learning. Standing back to write down the three or four learning points when a decision has gone well or badly is never wasted. We can so easily move remorselessly from one decision to another without ever taking stock and reflecting. Looking at three or four learning points rather than twenty-five can help us focus on next steps rather than being daunted by an excessively long list.

6. Be willing to make decisions

So often we can be caught in indecision where we keep going through the arguments again and again. Often we have to decide on the basis of partial information. Avoiding making a decision is making a decision not to take an action! The learning comes from making the decision, observing your own reaction and the responses of those around you, and then having the confidence to keep making decisions.

7. Grow your courage

Courage is the ability to step out into the unknown. Growing courage is not about becoming foolhardy; it is about seeing opportunities, assessing risks and being willing to take a consistent set of actions. Growing courage will involve both being aware of the perspective of others and sometimes developing a thicker skin, so that your courage is informed by but not quashed by the views of those around you.

8. Develop your communication skills

Becoming a better communicator as you make decisions starts from growing your listening, engaging and persuading skills without falling into the trap of appearing to manipulate. It is watching your words and expressions. It is fine tuning both the tone and content. So often an individual can win the argument but leave someone unpersuaded because their approach and demeanour have been dismissive.

9. Build sounding boards

The good decision maker will have built a sequence of sounding boards to test out their ideas. This may be a trusted colleague at work, a mentor who has wide experience or a coach who brings perspectives to bear from a wide variety of different worlds. Building good sounding boards is not about ducking responsibility; it is an individual recognising that their responsibilities are such that it is vital to triangulate their perspective with others and to view issues from a variety of perspectives. Hence the value of building a network of personal support covering wise people from both within and outside your particular sphere.

10. Obtain feedback

Good quality feedback given in a positive and supportive way is one of the most valuable gifts an individual can receive. It may involve seeking out individuals you trust whom you can ask directly for feedback, using an independent person like a coach to seek the perspective of others, or using a 360-degree feedback instrument. It is important to interpret feedback with care; not all feedback is accurate and may be distorted by the perspective of the observer. What matters is consciously deciding how you are going to embed the learning from feedback.

Developing Your Capacity to Make Hard Decisions: Christian Understanding and Skills

1. Embed the life and teaching of Jesus

The distinctiveness of the Christian perspective comes through embedding the life and teaching of Jesus. It is likely to involve reading and listening to sections from the Gospels on a regular basis so you are refreshed by the life, actions and words of Jesus. It is being open to the continued relevance of Gospel stories. It may mean asking yourself 'what would Jesus do?' in particular circumstances and seeing whether asking that question helps clarify principles that are relevant. Paul writes, 'as you received Christ Jesus the Lord so walk in him, rooted and built up in him' (Col. 2:6–7). Walking in Christ and aiming to embrace his approach through continually renewing our understanding of Jesus' life and teaching is the foundation stone for bringing a Christian perspective to decision making.

2. Reflect on Scripture

Sitting inside the biblical narrative in both the Old and New Testaments and visualising being present when decisions were made can enable us to understand more readily why decisions were made and to gain learning from the experiences of these individuals. For example, why did Moses, Abraham, Jonah and Paul make the decisions they did, and is that relevant to you? Reflecting on the Scriptures might mean absorbing the words of one of the Proverbs or part of a Psalm each day and letting its significance for you influence the decisions you make that day. It could mean reflecting on how the fruit of the Spirit, summarised by Paul as love, joy, peace, patience, kindness, goodness, faithfulness, gentleness and self-control, can influence the way we make decisions.

3. Nurture wisdom

The Old Testament includes a section called wisdom literature which is full of practical advice. The Psalmist exhorts, 'make me to know your ways O Lord: teach me your paths' (Ps. 25) and 'He leads me in the way of righteousness' (Ps. 23). Wisdom is seen as travelling along the right paths. J. I.

Packer and Carolyn Nystrom suggest that 'wisdom is indeed pragmatic . . . but it is humble, honest, realistic, insightful, generous, compassionate, stabilising and encouraging also'. The apostle James wrote about asking God for wisdom for he 'gives generously and without reproach' (James 1:5–6). So seeking and nurturing wisdom is an important part of developing the capacity to make good decisions.

4. Learn from role models

It can be helpful to reflect on decisions made by Christians in earlier generations and in the current era. William Wilberforce saw his calling as a Christian to be diligent in the business of life—hence his resolve to end the slave trade. Mother Teresa was determined to have a strong impact on reducing child poverty in India. Pioneers with a vision have brought focused energy to developing aid organisations. Learning from such leaders and being conscious of the long term impact they can have on others can provide a sense of inspiration when approaching decisions.

5. Recognise and use your gifts

The gifts we have are not to be ignored. Can we allow ourselves to believe that God has given us gifts that are there to be used? This is not about being proud or arrogant about our gifts; it is about using them in a constructive way. Allowing ourselves to be encouraged by the gifts we have been given, and how we have been able to use them in the past, is part of our thankfulness to God. A strong sense of humility is important, but failing to use our gifts of understanding or wisdom when asked to contribute to decisions is an abrogation of responsibility.

6. Listen to your heart

Sometimes we are troubled by a decision and have no inner peace about it. When we do have a sense of inner peace we are more likely to have reached the right decision. Paul told the Philippians, 'the peace of the Lord, which surpasses all understanding, will guard your hearts and minds in Christ Jesus' (Phil. 4:7). Gordon Smith writes that discernment is learnt over time as we come to recognise the movement of God in our hearts. He writes of coming with open hearts before the truth so that we are fully engaged with the Spirit of the Living God.

7. Engage with others

Learning through engaging with others is both about engaging with our natural allies and those with whom we differ in view or approach. Finding a mentor, coach or spiritual director who has experience of difficult decisions as a Christian can provide a sounding board and sense of encouragement. Jesus sent the disciples out in pairs, recognising their need for mutual encouragement and support. Sharpening our understanding also comes from engaging with those with whom we disagree, as Jesus did on frequent occasions.

8. Pray continually

If prayer is about being fully there in the presence of God, finding time and energy to be focused in prayer is a priority when decisions are to be made. It may be an opportunity to reflect quietly on how Jesus might have approached a situation or on the relevance of one of the key Christian themes like forgiveness, compassion, hope, new life or resurrection. Knowing what works best for you in a demanding period is important so that through your preferred pattern of thoughts or words you become more reflective, with the emotional clutter diminished and the clarity of your thinking and prayerfulness enhanced. Seeking greater wisdom through prayer is a perfectly legitimate request.

9. Spend time in a special space

One aspect of the Judeo-Christian perspective is the importance of special places. What are the spaces where your intellectual, emotional and spiritual resources are best in harmony together? It might be sitting inside a majestic cathedral, being silent in a small chapel, walking through fields, sitting in the garden or walking by pounding waves. When you need to make hard decisions, going to special places can put you in a frame of mind where you see the issues more clearly.

10. Be open to being surprised

The disciples were continually taken by surprise by the words and actions of Jesus and only gradually understood the full purpose of his ministry. As we prepare to make decisions an openness to being surprised can bring new insights and perspectives. What may be needed is a combination of places and routines we know well, alongside an openness to new thinking. Do allow yourself to be surprised by what you see and observe, and then view those surprises as if the risen Christ is alongside you. Be ready for your understanding of God's purposes to continue to grow as you are open to the God who has created us, to Jesus whose life and work continues to be relevant today, and to the Holy Spirit who is never far from us.

Conclusion

There are important pitfalls to watch:

- beware of those playing the 'God card' as a means of avoiding the issue and trying to get their own way;

- do not assume that a Christian perspective makes it easier to make decisions: it can make it harder because you see a wider set of perspectives;

- watch when fear or apprehension gets in the way and begins to distort your perspective; and

- beware of believing that using your mental and emotional gifts when weighing up a decision is somehow a poorer approach than direct ministry from the Holy Spirit. The Holy Spirit of God normally works through our mental faculties and not contrary to them.

Drawing from both our human and Christian experiences is about allowing ourselves to be transformed so that hard decisions do not fill us with fear. Progress is about being able to step out believing we can make hard decisions that are true to our values. We should never expect it to become easy to make hard decisions. If making hard decisions were easy we would not be doing it well. A touch of uncertainty or vulnerability is vital to keep our level of sensitivity high so that we never become complacent when hard decisions have to be made.

Key questions to reflect on might be:

- Which of the points above resonate most for you?
- How might you take forward three of them over the next few months?
- Who can you share this with who will hold you to account in developing your capacity to make decisions?

Next Steps

What a privilege it is to be asked to make decisions. They may sometimes seem demanding and eat up our energy but the ability to make decisions is a gift God has given to us. It is a responsibility to be taken thoughtfully, prayerfully, reflectively and then decisively with an understanding of the impact that decisions have on those affected.

As we reflect on Jesus as leader we can embrace his boldness, commitment, resoluteness and clarity as well as follow his example of selectivity in his use of time, his availability to people and his patience as he waited for the right moment for action.

My hope for you is that as you make decisions you are able to embrace the teaching of Jesus to be as wise as serpents and as innocent as doves. May we be known for wisdom and a sense of perspective that is rooted in Christian understanding and helps make a significant difference both to the way decisions are made and the decisions themselves.

Appendix: An Illustrative Outline for a Workshop on *Deciding Well*

Outcomes

- to be clear about how you are going to develop your capacity to make hard decisions
- to work through some specific decisions

Sequence of Workshop

- Jesus' approach to making decisions, with a particular focus on his words, 'be as wise as serpents and as innocent as doves' (chapter 1)
- Sharing of observations about who makes decisions well and how do they do it (chapter 2)
- What is Christian discernment and what is its relevance to the way we make decisions? (chapter 3)
- Sharing of current approaches to decision making by participants (chapter 4)
- Looking at key questions in making decisions (chapter 5)

- Addressing specific types of decisions such as strategic priorities, short term priorities, the use of time and energy, management issues, and choices about next steps (chapter 6)
- Working through the approaches suggested in the book for developing your capacity to make hard decisions, first in terms of general understanding and skills and then in terms of Christian understanding (chapter 7), as well as looking at additional ideas from participants
- Commitments from individuals about their own next steps

Bibliography

Bibb, Sally, and Jeremy Koudri. *Trust Matters: For Organisation and Personal Success*. Basingstoke: Palgrave Macmillan, 2004.

Buford, Bob. *Stuck at Half-time*. Grand Rapids: Zondervan, 2001.

France, R. T. *The Gospel according to Matthew*. Tyndale New Testament Commentaries. Grand Rapids: Wm. B. Eerdmans, 1985.

Hammond, John S., Ralph L. Keeney, and Howard Raiffa. *Smart Choices: A Practical Guide to Making Better Life Decisions*. New York: Broadway Books, 1999.

Hirst, Judy. *Struggling to be Holy*. London: Darton, Longman and Todd, 2006.

Lewis, C. S. *Mere Christianity*. London: Fount, 1997.

Nouwen, Henri. *In the Name of Jesus: Reflections on Christian Leadership*. New York: Crossroad, 1989.

———. *Bread for the Journey*. London: Darton, Longman and Todd, 1996.

Packer, J. I., and Carolyn Nystrom. *Guard Us, Guide Us: Divine Leading and Life's Decisions*. Grand Rapids: Baker Books, 2008.

Shaw, Peter A. *Making Difficult Decisions: How to be Decisive and Get the Business Done*. Chichester: Capstone, 2008.

Smith, Gordon T. *The Voice of Jesus: Discernment, Prayers, and the Witness of the Spirit*. Downers Grove: InterVarsity Press, 2003.

Waltke, Bruce K. *Finding the Will of God: A Pagan Notion?* Grand Rapids and Cambridge: Wm. B. Eerdmans; Vancouver: Regent College Publishing, 1995.

Watson, Andrew. *The Fourfold Leadership of Jesus.* Abingdon: Bible Reading Fellowship, 2008.

Wright, N. T. *Matthew for Everyone.* Vol. 1. London: SPCK Publishing, 2002.

Other Books by Peter Shaw

Mirroring Jesus as Leader. Cambridge: Grove, 2004.

Conversation Matters: How to Engage Effectively With One Another. London: Continuum, 2005.

The Four Vs of Leadership: Vision, Values, Value-added, Vitality. Chichester: Capstone, 2006.

Finding Your Future: The Second Time Around. London: Darton, Longman and Todd, 2006.

Business Coaching: Achieving Practical Results through Effective Engagement. Chichester: Capstone, 2007. (Co-authored with Robin Linnecar)

Making Difficult Decisions: How to Be Decisive and Get the Business Done. Chichester: Capstone, 2008.

Riding the Rapids: How to Navigate through Turbulent Times. London: Praesta, 2008. (Co-authored with Jane Stephens)

Raise Your Game: Achieving Your Full Potential. Chichester: Capstone, 2009 (forthcoming).

The Christian Leader in the Secular World of Work. Colorado Springs: Authentic, 2010 (forthcoming).

Defining Moments. Basingstoke: Palgrave Macmillan, 2010 (forthcoming).

Printed in the United Kingdom by
Lightning Source UK Ltd., Milton Keynes
139000UK00001B/4/P